The Moonlight Orchestra

Happy House

About Wise & Wide

- A systematic 6-level English reading program based on Lexile® measures
- Diverse and interesting topics chosen from the elementary curriculums of Korea and English speaking western countries
- Well-written books in various forms including fiction stories, descriptive texts, and classics retold
- The informative but original fiction stories grab your interest, leading to the easy and clear understanding of the educational content.
- Improve thinking skills with solid after-reading activities at all levels of the series.

Wise & Wide is a 6-level English reading program that consists of 60 books and each level is systematically divided by Lexile® measures. The Lexile® Framework for Reading is the most popular reading measuring system in American formal education curriculums and many English programs. Over 20 out of 50 states in the U.S. mark Lexile® measures directly on students' final report cards and over 300 well-known publishers adopt and use Lexile® measures.

Experience many kinds of readings written by professional writers from the U.S. and England. They used interesting topics that were carefully chosen after analyzing elementary curriculums from around the world including Korea, the U.S., England, and Australia among many others. Comprehensive after-reading activities including graphic organizers, speaking tasks, and After-reading Tests are ready for you.

Levels in the series and their corresponding Lexile® measures

Level	Lexile® measures	U.S. Grade
Level 1	Below 200L	Pre K - K
Level 2	190L - 400L	Lower Grade 1
Level 3	350L - 530L	Upper Grade 1
Level 4	420L - 650L	Grade 2
Level 5	520L - 940L	Grade 3 - 4
Level 6	830L - 1070L	Grade 5 - 6

* Smart Readers: Wise & Wide level 1 is applicable to the preschool level in the U.S.
* The source of the relationship between Lexile® measures and U.S. school grades: CCSS(Common Core State Standards) FOR ENGLISH LANGUAGE ARTS, APPENDIX A (2012, which is used by 45 states in the U.S.)

Topic List

	Level 1	Level 2	Level 3	Level 4	Level 5	Level 6
Book 1	Science>Biology: The hibernation of animals Story	Science>Biology: Living and nonliving things Story	Science>Biology> Animals & the Environment: Sea otters Story	Environment> Living with nature: The diver & the persimmon tree Story	Science>Biology> Animal: Amazing animals of the Amazon Story	Science>Biology: Germs, transmitted diseases Story
Book 2	Literature> World classics: Aesop's fables Story	Literature> Traditional fairy tale: Old tales about stones Story	Social Studies> Economy: To run a business to make and save money Story	Science>Biology> Plants: Photosynthesis Story	Science>Earth science: Earth's layers, earthquakes, volcanoes, and earth's atmosphere Report	Mathematics> Sequence: The golden ratio & the Fibonacci sequence Story
Book 3	Science>Physics: How shadows are formed Story	Literature> World classics: Peter Pan Story	Science>Scientific technology: Nanobots Story	Literature>Myths: World's creation stories Story	Literature> Legend: The story of King Arthur Story	Literature>Myths: Constellation myths Story
Book 4	Literature> Traditional literature: The Talmud Story	Science>Biology> Animal: Polar bears Story	Science>Biology> Animal: Mountain gorillas Story	Social Studies> Cultural anthropology: Amazing ancient cultures of the world Story	Science> Earth science: Clouds and weather Story	Literature> Human & animals: The friendship between a girl and a horse Story
Book 5	Social Studies> Ethics: Rules in daily life Story	Science>Biology: The five senses Report	Social Studies> Cultural anthropology: Astonishing festivals Report	Art>Music: Stories from two operas Story	Social Studies> World culture & history: The Renaissance Story	Sports> Board sports: Surfing & snowboarding Story
Book 6	Social Studies> World geography & travel: Tourist attractions around the world Story	Science>Biology> Animal: Dinosaurs Story	Science> Astronomy: The solar system Story	Social Studies> People: Three great people who overcame hardships Story	Science>Scientific technology: The wonderful world of robots Report	Art>Music: Composers of the Romantic Era Report
Book 7	Science> Space science: The life of astronauts Report	Social Studies> Cultural anthropology: Mythological monsters from around the world Report	Mathematics> Elementary mathematics: Numbers, measurement, shapes and data Report	Science & Social Studies> Technology & culture: Inventions from around the world Report	Art>Works of art: Famous paintings Report	Social Studies> Human & animals: Animals in action for human Report
Book 8	Social Studies> Cultural anthropology: Various living cultures of the world Story	Art>Music: Instruments in the orchestra Story	Social Studies> Life safety: Learning and using outdoor survival skills Story	Social Studies> History: The California Gold Rush Report	Social Studies & Science> Psychology: Psychology in everyday life Story	Literature> World classics: The Merchant of Venice Story
Book 9	Social Studies> Jobs: Interviews about jobs Report	Science>Scientific technology: Developments in technology in different times Story	Social Studies> Politics>Election: Running for 3rd grade class president Story	Literature> World classics: Stories of Sherlock Holmes Story	Literature> World classics: Adrift in the Pacific Story	
Book 10		Sports>Winter sports: Various aspects of some Winter Olympic sports Report				

* 10 books in each level will be published.

How to Use This Book

•Before Reading

You can easily find the topic and what kind of story you are about to read.

•The text

All the stories were written by professional writers from the U.S. and England, so you will read authentic and appropriate English sentences and expressions in every book in the series.

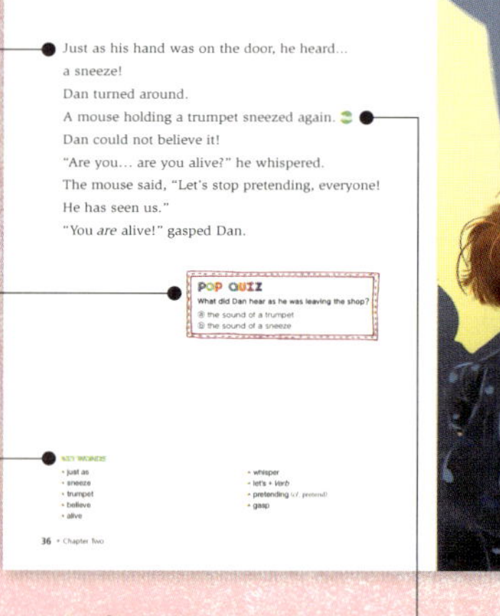

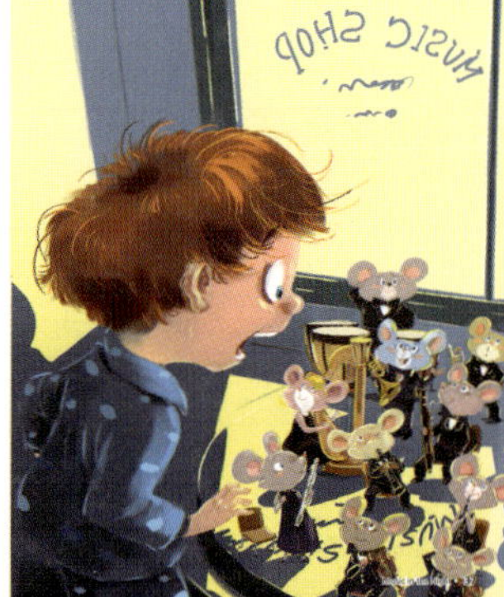

•Pop Quiz

Check out right away if you understand what you have just read by solving a pop quiz that checks your comprehension.

•Key Words

The key words and expressions on each page are listed for you to easily study them.

•Aha! Tips

Download free Korean explanations at *www.ihappyhouse.co.kr* for all of the sentences marked with "Aha!". These explain cultural, scientific, and economic knowledge or they deal with aspects of English such as grammatical structures or idiomatic expressions. There are lots of "Aha! Tips" to help you understand the text.

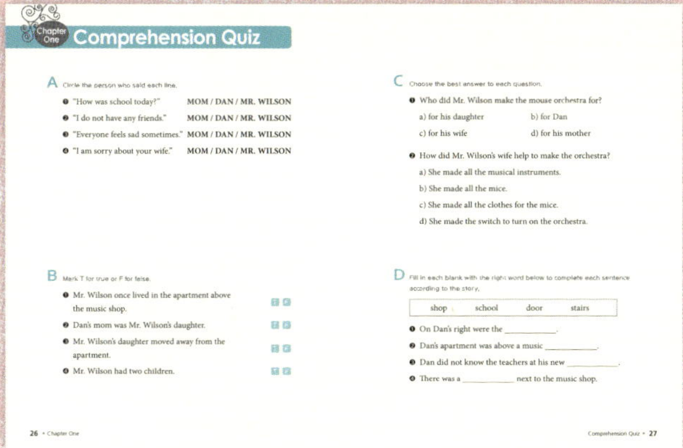

•Comprehension Quiz

After reading one chapter, solve various questions to find out if you fully understand the content.

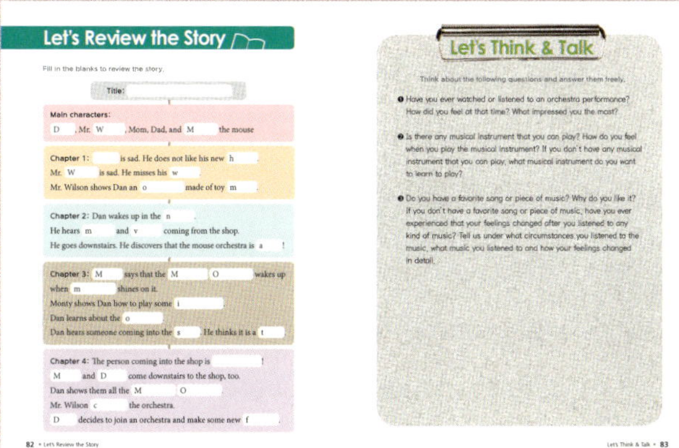

•Let's Review the Story /
•Let's Think & Talk

Fill in the blanks in the organizer to summarize the whole story. Express your own thinking and feelings about the story by answering the questions. You can build up logic and reasoning skills for your essay examinations in the future.

Appendix

Audio CD

In the CD audio book form, the texts are read vividly by American professional voice actors.
(MP3 files downloaded for free)

After-reading Test

Solve an additionally provided After-reading Test for each book.

The Korean translation, Answer Keys, a Word Quiz, a Word List, and Aha! Tips for each book

You can download them for free at *www.ihappyhouse.co.kr* or *www.darakwon.co.kr*

Before Reading

The Moonlight Orchestra

Level 2–8,
Lexile® 300L

•Art⟩Music
•Story

Playing together makes music more beautiful!

Have you ever listened an orchestra play a concert? Musicians play many different kinds of instruments such as string, woodwind, brass, and percussion instruments. They gather together and play music under the baton of a conductor. The music comes from everyone's collaborative effort and it deeply moves listeners by comforting the sorrowful mind, healing the wounded mind, and adding vigor and energy to the cheerful mind. The power of music is so great and mysterious that it can do many things.

In the book, you meet a lonely main character who comforts his mind with music. Then, he is determined to have a fresh start. Let's read about the amazing friends he makes and learn about all the different kinds of orchestra instruments that can make beautiful music.

Summary

Dan who has recently moved to an unfamiliar town is gloomy. All he can see are unfamiliar faces and places. There are no friends at school and no teachers whom he is familiar with, so it isn't fun for him. How he wishes he could live in the town he used to live in!

One night, Dan is woken up by a strange noise. Then he hears more noises. It seems that they are coming from the music store downstairs. But it is the middle of the night and the store is closed, so no one is there. What on earth are those sounds coming from the empty music store? Hesitating Dan takes his courage and opens the door of the music store... Oh my God! He sees a scene so amazing that he can't believe it!

Contents

The Moonlight Orchestra

The Moonlight Orchestra

A Sad Song

Dan stood by the window of a music shop.

He looked at his reflection in the window.

His face looked sad. Aha!

He and his parents had just moved to a new home.

He did not like his new home.

He did not like his new school.

He did not like his new town.

He wished that he still lived in his old home.

He wished that he still went to his old school.

He wished that he still lived in his old town.

He lived with his family in an apartment.

The apartment was above the music shop.

KEY WORDS

- sad
- **stand** (stand-stood-stood)
- **by the window of**
- **music shop** (*cf.* music)
- **look at** (*cf.* look)
- reflection
- move to
- like

- town
- wish
- still
- live
- **go to school** (go-went-gone)
- apartment
- above

Mom looked down from upstairs.

"Dan!" she called.

"How was school today?"

Dan shook his head.

"I did not like it."

"Why not?"

"I do not have any friends. Aha!

I do not know the teachers."

Mom made a sad face.

"It will get better, Dan.

I promise that it will get better.

It just takes time to get used to a new place."

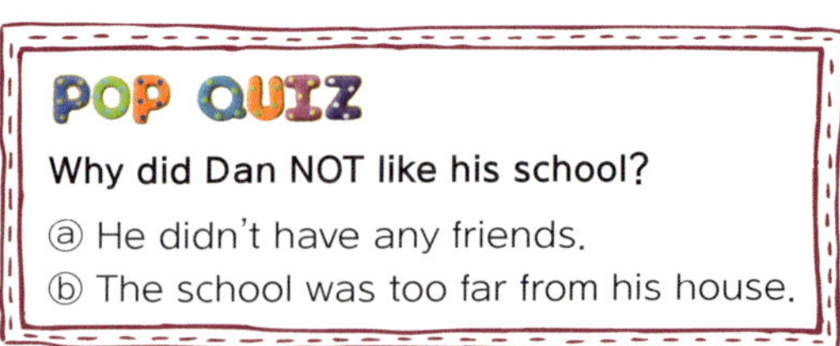

KEY WORDS

- look down
- upstairs
- call
- shake one's head (shake-shook-shaken)
- Why not?

- make a sad face (make-made-made)
- get better (get-got-gotten)
- promise
- take time to + *Verb* (take-took-taken)
- get used to

MUSIC SHOP
MUSIC SHOP

There was a door next to the music shop. Aha!

Behind the door was a hallway.

Some stairs led up from the hallway.

The stairs led up to Dan's apartment.

Dan went to open the door.

Suddenly there was a loud KNOCK-KNOCK-
KNOCK.

Dan jumped.

Someone was knocking on the window of the music shop.

It was the old man who owned the shop.

His name was Mr. Wilson.

"Come inside," said Mr. Wilson.

Dan did not want to go inside.

He wanted to go home.

But Mr. Wilson smiled and picked up a violin.

"Come and listen," he said.

KEY WORDS

- next to
- behind
- hallway
- stairs
- lead (lead-led-led)

- suddenly
- loud
- knock
- jump
- own

- inside (↔ outside)
- smile
- pick up
- violin
- listen

So Dan went into the shop.

Mr. Wilson began to play his violin. Dan listened to the music. It was a sad song.

It made Dan want to cry. **Aha!**

"Why do you play such sad music?" asked Dan.

Mr. Wilson smiled again.

"When I play the music, the sadness comes out of me and into the music. It makes me feel better."

Dan looked at Mr. Wilson.

His hair was gray and his clothes were worn.

"Have you ever felt sad?" asked Dan.

"Of course I have," said Mr. Wilson.

"Everyone feels sad sometimes.

But music is a good way to let your feelings out."

POP QUIZ

According to the story, match the two sides correctly.

ⓐ Mr. Wilson's hair was   •   • ① worn.
ⓑ Mr. Wilson's clothes were •   • ② gray.

KEY WORDS

- **gray** (= grey)
- **worn**
- **Have you ever + *p.p.* ~?**

- **of course**
- **everyone**
- **sometimes**

- **a good way to**
- **let ~ out** (let-let-let)
- **feelings** (*cf.* feeling)

Dan looked around the shop.

In the window, there was a group of toy mice.

There were fifteen of them.

They all sat in a circle.

Each mouse held an instrument.

Each mouse wore tiny clothes.

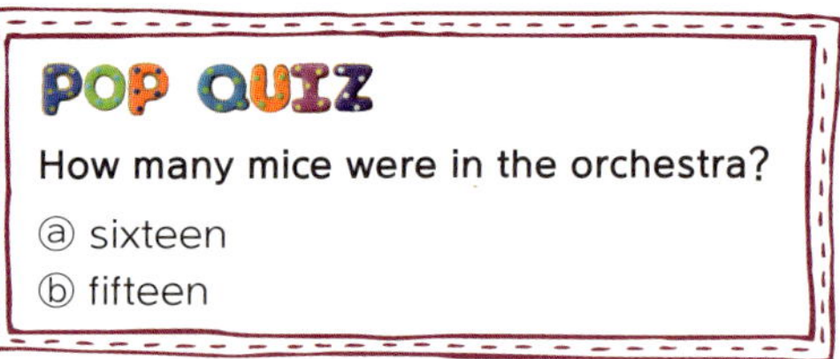

- look around
- a group of
- mice
- sit (sit-sat-sat)
- in a circle
- each
- hold (hold-held-held)

- instrument (= musical instrument)
- wear (wear-wore-worn)
- tiny
- orchestra
- press
- switch
- beside

"What is this?" asked Dan.

"This is my mouse orchestra," said Mr. Wilson. 

"Watch this."

He pressed a switch beside the window.

The toy mice began to move.

Each one played its instrument.

Dan smiled and clapped his hands.

"That is so clever!" he said.

"I made it for my daughter," said Mr. Wilson.

"My wife stitched all the clothes."

His smile went away.

He looked sad again.

"Why are you sad?" asked Dan.

"I used to live above this shop," said Mr. Wilson. Aha!

KEY WORDS

- clap one's hands
- clever
- daughter (*cf.* son)
- stitch
- go away
- That's right.
- if
- through
- point
- at the back of
- open onto

"In my apartment?" asked Dan.

"Yes, that's right.

If you go through that door, it leads to the stairs."

He pointed to a door that was at the back of the shop.

"Oh, yes," said Dan.

"I have seen that door.

It opens onto my hallway."

Mr. Wilson switched off the mouse orchestra.

The mice were still.

The music stopped.

"I lived there with my wife and my daughter,"
said Mr. Wilson.

"Then, my daughter grew up.

She moved away.

Only my wife and I were left."

"Where is your wife now?" asked Dan.

"She died last year," said Mr. Wilson.

"Now, I live with my daughter on the other side of town."

"Why don't you live in the apartment?" asked Dan.

"It is too sad for me," said Mr. Wilson.

"I don't want to live there without my wife. It should have a family living in it."

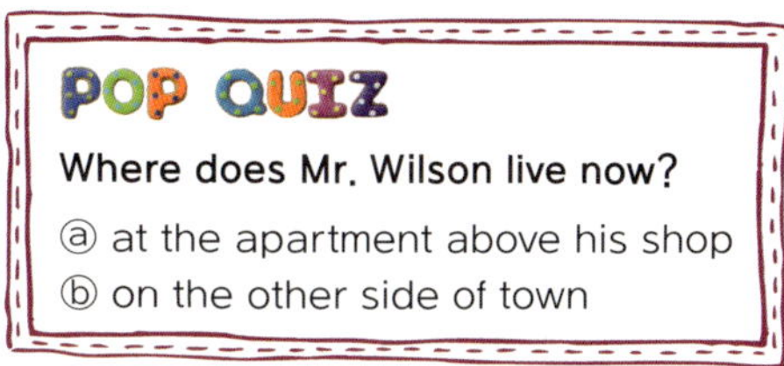

KEY WORDS

- **switch off** (↔ switch on)
- **then**
- **grow up** (grow-grew-grown)
- **move away**
- **be left**
- **die**

- **last year**
- **on the other side of** (*cf.* other)
- **why don't you ~?**
- **without** (↔ with)
- **should**

Dan heard Mom calling. **Aha!**

"I am sorry about your wife," he said.

"I have to go."

"You can use this door," said Mr. Wilson.

He unlocked the door at the back of the shop.

Dan went through it.

He was in the hallway.

On his left was the door to the street.

On his right were the stairs.

Dan went up the stairs to the apartment.

When he reached the top, he turned to listen.

Mr. Wilson was playing his violin again.

The sad song followed Dan up the stairs.

Comprehension Quiz

A Circle the person who said each line.

❶ "How was school today?" **MOM / DAN / MR. WILSON**

❷ "I do not have any friends." **MOM / DAN / MR. WILSON**

❸ "Everyone feels sad sometimes." **MOM / DAN / MR. WILSON**

❹ "I am sorry about your wife." **MOM / DAN / MR. WILSON**

B Mark T for true or F for false.

❶ Mr. Wilson once lived in the apartment above the music shop. T F

❷ Dan's mom was Mr. Wilson's daughter. T F

❸ Mr. Wilson's daughter moved away from the apartment. T F

❹ Mr. Wilson had two children. T F

C Choose the best answer to each question.

❶ Who did Mr. Wilson make the mouse orchestra for?

   a) for his daughter   b) for Dan

   c) for his wife   d) for his mother

❷ How did Mr. Wilson's wife help to make the orchestra?

   a) She made all the musical instruments.

   b) She made all the mice.

   c) She made all the clothes for the mice.

   d) She made the switch to turn on the orchestra.

D Fill in each blank with the right word below to complete each sentence according to the story.

shop	school	door	stairs

❶ On Dan's right were the _______________.

❷ Dan's apartment was above a music _______________.

❸ Dan did not know the teachers at his new _______________.

❹ There was a _______________ next to the music shop.

Chapter Two

Music in the Night

Dan woke up.

He had heard a strange noise.

It was the middle of the night.

He was in his bed.

He listened.

Mom and Dad were asleep in the next room.

Dad was snoring.

Perhaps Dad's snoring had woken him.

Dan lay down again.

Then, he heard the strange noise again.

It was coming from the shop below.

KEY WORDS

- **wake up** (wake-woke-woken)
- **strange**
- **noise**
- **the middle of the night**
- **asleep**
- **snore**

- **perhaps**
- **snoring**
- **lie down** (lie-lay-lain)
- **come from**
- **below**

He listened.

It was a scratching noise.

There was also the sound of tiny voices.

Then, he heard music.

It was very, very quiet.

Perhaps Mr. Wilson had left his radio on.

Dan got up.

"I will go down and switch off the radio," he said. Aha!

KEY WORDS

- scratch
- sound
- voice
- quiet (*cf.* quietly)
- leave ~ on (leave-left-left)
- get up
- go down

- go out of
- be locked
- could
- clearly
- tune
- squeaky
- laugh (*cf.* laughter)

He went out of his bedroom.

He went down the stairs.

He went to open the door to the shop.

But the door was locked.

Now, he could hear the noise more clearly.

The music was a happy tune.

The voices were high and squeaky.

They were laughing.

Dan tried to open the door.

He pushed it and he shook the door handle.

The voices stopped.

"That is very strange," thought Dan.

"The radio has switched itself off."

He stepped away from the door.

He started to climb the stairs.

The voices and laughter began again.

Dan stopped.

He turned around and he went back to the door.

Then, he saw a key.

It was hanging on a hook by the door.

POP QUIZ

According to the story, match the two sides correctly.

ⓐ When Dan shook the door handle,　·　　·　① the voices stopped.
ⓑ When Dan started to climb the stairs, ·　　·　② the voices began again.

KEY WORDS

- try
- push (↔ pull)
- handle
- think (think-thought-thought)
- itself
- step away from

- climb
- turn around
- hang on (hang-hung-hung)
- hook
- with a click
- creep (creep-crept-crept)

Dan tried the key in the lock.

Very, very quietly, he turned the key.

With a *click*, the door opened.

Dan crept through the door.

He went into the shop.

There, in the window, was the mouse orchestra.
Moonlight shone through the window onto the
mice.

Some were playing their musical instruments.

Some were talking.

Some were laughing.

Mr. Wilson must have left it switched on! Aha!

Dan laughed out loud.

At once, the voices stopped.

The music stopped, too.

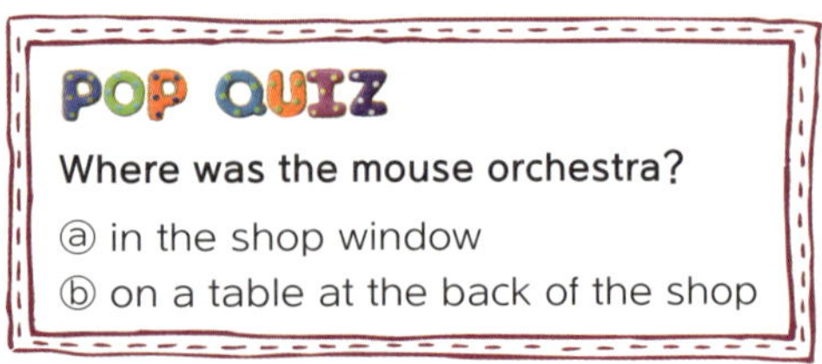

Dan walked over to the mouse orchestra.

His heart was beating very fast.

The mice were still.

Nothing moved.

"I must have imagined it," thought Dan.

He checked that the switch was off.

He turned to leave.

KEY WORDS

- moonlight
- **shine** (shine-shone-shone)
- must
- out loud

- at once
- walk over to
- heart
- **beat** (beat-beat-beaten)

- nothing
- imagine
- check

Just as his hand was on the door, he heard…

a sneeze!

Dan turned around.

A mouse holding a trumpet sneezed again. 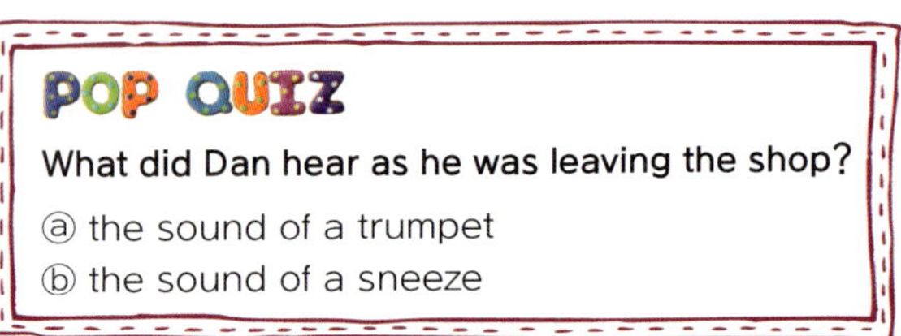

Dan could not believe it!

"Are you… are you alive?" he whispered.

The mouse said, "Let's stop pretending, everyone!

He has seen us."

"You *are* alive!" gasped Dan.

POP QUIZ

What did Dan hear as he was leaving the shop?

ⓐ the sound of a trumpet
ⓑ the sound of a sneeze

KEY WORDS

- just as
- sneeze
- trumpet
- believe
- alive

- whisper
- let's + *Verb*
- pretending (*cf.* pretend)
- gasp

MUSIC SHOP

A  Mark T for true or F for false.

❶ A radio in the shop was switched on.　　　T　F

❷ Mr. Wilson had left the mouse orchestra switched on.　　　T　F

❸ The mice laughed and talked.　　　T　F

❹ A mouse with a violin sneezed.　　　T　F

B Fill in each blank with the right word below to complete each sentence according to the story.

started	thought	turned	crept

❶ Dan ______________ that the radio had switched itself off.

❷ Dan ______________ to climb the stairs.

❸ Dan ______________ around and he went back to the door.

❹ Dan ______________ through the door.

  Choose the best answer to each question.

❶ Who or what did Dan think was making the noise downstairs?

a) thieves

b) a mouse

c) a radio

d) Mr. Wilson

❷ How did Dan see the mice in the dark?

a) He switched on the lights.

b) He shone a flashlight onto them.

c) Moonlight shone onto them.

d) They glowed in the dark.

❸ What did the mouse with the trumpet tell the other mice to do?

a) stay still

b) play some music

c) start sneezing

d) stop pretending

Chapter Three

Mice and Music

"Yes, of course we are," said the mouse with the trumpet.

"My name is Monty.

We are the Moonlight Orchestra.

When the moonlight comes in through the window, it wakes us.

It makes us want to play music.

We play because we are happy.

Or sometimes we play because we are sad.

But we only play in the moonlight.

Only the person who needs us can hear us." Aha!

KEY WORDS

- only
- person
- need

MUSIC SHOP
MUSIC SHOP

"But how… what…?" Dan was so surprised that he could not speak. 

All the mice were stretching and moving about now.

"Do you know much about music?" asked Monty.

"No," said Dan.

"I tried to play the piano once, but I could not read the music."

"You do not have to read music," said Monty.

"You can still enjoy it. You only need to listen."

Dan's bare feet were cold, but he did not care.

This was the most amazing thing that he had ever seen!

"Have you ever played the trumpet?" asked Monty.

"No, I have never played the trumpet," said Dan.

"Then why not try?" said Monty.

He pointed toward a shiny instrument hanging on the wall.

"Mr. Wilson will not mind."

KEY WORDS

- surprised
- stretch
- move about
- much
- once
- **read** (read-read-read)

- enjoy
- bare
- feet
- care
- amazing
- thing

- never
- toward
- shiny
- mind

Dan took the trumpet down.

"I do not know how to play it."

"Watch me," said Monty.

Monty put his trumpet to his lips.

Dan did the same.

Monty puffed out his cheeks.

Dan did the same.

Monty blew into his trumpet.

Dan did the same.

A horrible noise came out of the end.

It sounded like an angry elephant.

All the mice laughed.

"Maybe the trumpet is not the right instrument

for you," said Monty.

"But listen to the brass section of our orchestra."

KEY WORDS

- take down
- how to + *Verb*
- same
- puff out
- blow into
  (blow-blew-blown)
- horrible
- come out (of)
- end
- sound like
- maybe
- brass section
  (*cf.* brass / section)

▲ a cornetist and a tubaist
playing their instruments

Four other mice stepped forward.

Each one held an instrument made of shiny brass.

Each instrument had a mouthpiece to blow into.

Each instrument had a large opening at the other end.

The sound came out of it.

"That is called the bell," explained Monty. Aha!

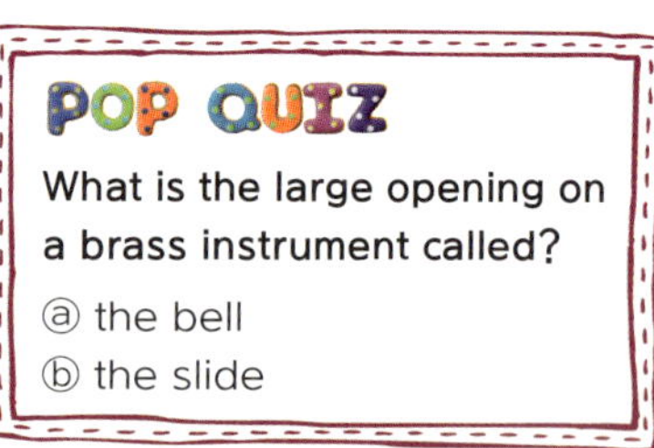

"My name is Tom," said a
mouse.
"I play the trombone."
The trombone had a
long piece of brass.
Tom moved it
backward and forward
with his paw.

"This is the slide.
It changes the pitch of the note."
"What is the pitch?" asked Dan.
"It means how high or low the note is," explained
Tom.

KEY WORDS

- trombone
- piece
- backward (↔ forward)
- paw
- slide

- change
- pitch
- note
- mean (mean-meant-meant)

"Listen to this."

Tom blew into his trombone.

It made a high, squeaky sound.

He moved the slide away from his body.

The sound got lower and lower.

The other mice with brass instruments began to play a tune.

Monty joined in on his trumpet.

The cornet made a high sound.

The tuba made a low sound.

One mouse had a horn.

It made a very soft sound.

Together, the brass instruments made wonderful music.

The low notes and the high notes worked together perfectly.

▲ a hornist playing the horn

"You can play music with other people," said Monty.

"It sounds better together.

It is a good way of making new friends."

Dan remembered that he had no friends here.

He missed his old friends.

He felt sad again.

Dan put the trumpet back.

"I will try another instrument," he said.

"I will try the violin."

KEY WORDS

- make friends
- remember
- have no friend

- miss
- put back (put-put-put)
- another

He lifted a violin off a shelf.

He picked up the bow.

He put the violin
under his chin.
"I saw Mr.
Wilson play
it," he said.
"I know what
to do." 
Dan tried to
play the violin.

He pulled and pushed
the bow across the violin's strings.

A horrible noise filled the shop.

It sounded like a screeching cat.

KEY WORDS

- lift
- shelf
- bow

- under
- chin
- string

- fill
- screeching

"Stop, stop, please stop!" yelled Monty.

"Let us show you what stringed instruments *should* sound like." 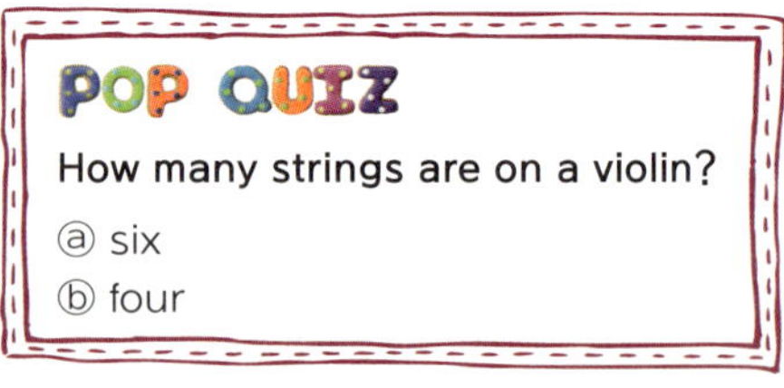

"Stringed instruments?" said Dan.

"What are they?"

"Look at your violin," said Monty.

"It has four strings on it.

The thicker strings make lower notes.

The thinner strings make higher notes.

You can make the strings tighter or looser.

That changes the notes, too."

Dan plucked the strings with his fingers.

It sounded better than when he used the bow.

"What other stringed instruments are there?" he asked.

KEY WORDS

- yell
- stringed
- thicker
- thinner
- tighter
- looser
- pluck
- finger

Monty clapped his paws together.

"Let us see the string section," he said.

He pointed at some mice.

One held a violin.

It was just like Dan's, but much smaller.

It was even smaller than his smallest finger.

The second mouse held an instrument that looked like a violin.

But it was a bit bigger.

"That one is a viola," explained Monty.

"It plays lower notes than the violin."

▲ a cellist playing the cello

KEY WORDS

- smaller
- even
- smallest
- look like
- a bit
- bigger
- viola
- cello
- sit down
- fit (fit-fit-fit)
- between
- knee
- draw (draw-drew-drawn)

"Mine is a cello," said another mouse, who was sitting down.

"My cello is so big that I must sit down to play it. It will not fit under my chin!"

The cello fit between her knees.

She drew the bow across the strings.

A beautiful low sound came out.

The last stringed instrument was even bigger than
the cello.

It was taller than the mouse that held it.

It rested on the ground and the mouse stood up
to play it.

"This is a double bass," said Monty.

"It can be played with a bow.

But often the player plucks the strings."

He reached over and plucked a string with his
fingers.

It made the lowest note of all.

"There is also my harp," said a soft voice.

"My name is Harriet."

Harriet leaned forward in her chair.

She ran her fingers across the harp strings.

The music sounded like rippling water.

"It sounds magical," said Dan.

"Music has its own magic," agreed Harriet.

"It can change your feelings.

It can make you remember good times.

It can help you to imagine things."

▲ a double bass and a harp

▲ a double bassist playing the double bass
by plucking the strings with his fingertips

KEY WORDS

- taller
- rest
- on the ground
- stand up
- double bass
- often
- lowest
- harp
- lean forward
- run (run-ran-run)
- ripple
- magical (*cf.* magic)
- good times

Dan felt a wave of sadness wash over him.

"Can it help me to like this place?"

Harriet opened her mouth to answer.

But, at that moment, a cloud passed in front of the moon.

The moonlight disappeared.

The shop went dark.

The Moonlight Orchestra was still.

It was only a group of toy mice, stiff and silent.

But not everything was silent.

Out on the dark street, footsteps were coming.

The footsteps came to the door, where they stopped.

The door rattled.

Someone was trying to get into the shop!

"It is a thief," thought Dan.

"I must raise the alarm!"

KEY WORDS

- a wave of (*cf*. wave)
- wash over
- at that moment
- in front of
- disappear
- go dark
- stiff
- silent
- footstep
- rattle
- thief (*cf*. thieves)
- raise the alarm

A Who said what? Match each line with the right character.

 **❶** 

Dan

❷

Harriet

❸ 

Monty

- a) "Music has its own magic."

- b) "You do not have to read music."

- c) "I tried to play the piano once."

B Put the sentences in order.

❶ Dan blew into the trumpet.

❷ A horrible noise came out.

❸ Dan put the trumpet to his lips.

❹ Dan puffed out his cheeks.

________ → ________ → ________ → ________

Choose the best answer to each question.

❶ Why did Dan's parents NOT hear the music of the Moonlight Orchestra?

a) They slept very deeply.

b) The noise did not reach the apartment above.

c) Only the person who needed to hear the music could hear it.

d) They were out for the evening.

❷ How did Dan know how to play the violin?

a) He had read a book about it.

b) Monty showed him how to play it.

c) He had played it before.

d) He had seen Mr. Wilson play it.

❸ Why did the orchestra suddenly become still?

a) A cloud hid the moon.

b) Dan switched it off.

c) A thief came into the shop.

d) Mom and Dad came downstairs.

Chapter Four

Sharing the Secret

The door creaked open.

A dark shape stood at the entrance to the shop.

Dan rushed over to a drum kit that stood at the back of the shop.

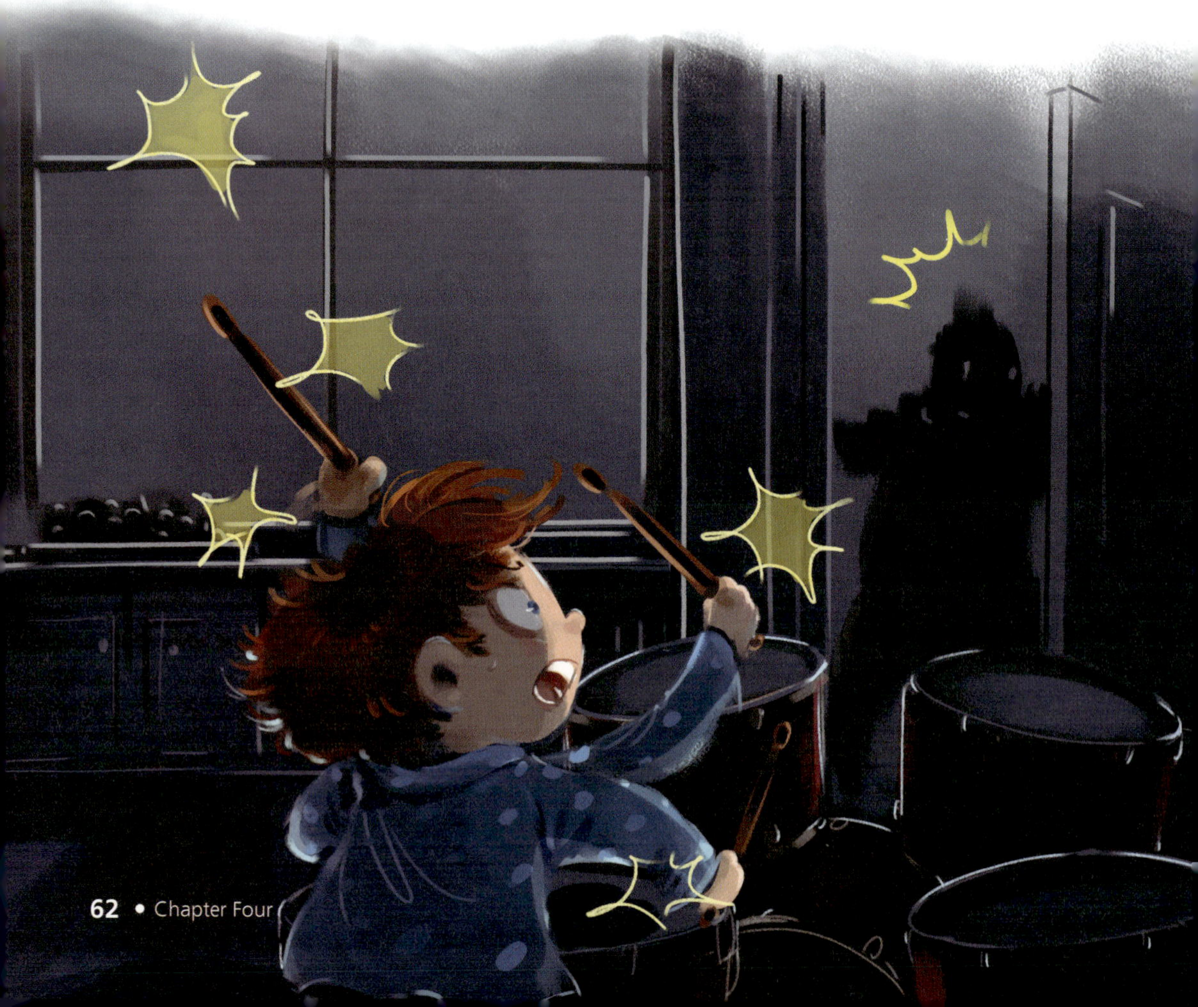

He picked up the drumsticks.

He hit the drums as hard as he could. **Aha!**

BANG! BASH! CLANG! CRASH!

The shape at the door jumped in fright.

"What on earth is that?" cried a man's voice.

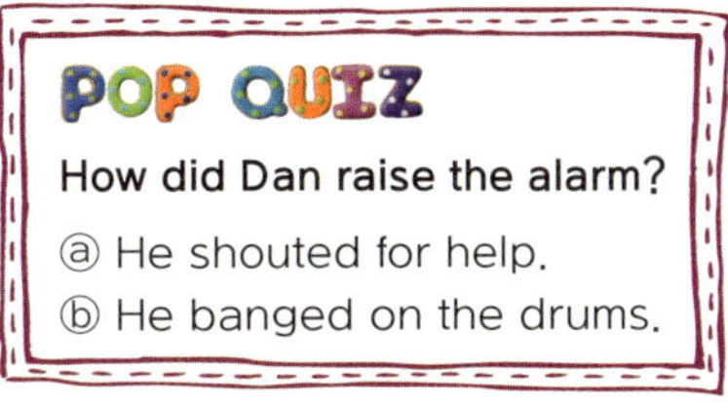

KEY WORDS

- share
- secret
- creak
- shape
- entrance
- rush
- drum
- kit
- drumstick

- hit (hit-hit-hit)
- hard
- bang
- bash
- clang
- crash
- in fright
- what on earth ~?

"Mr. Wilson!" gasped Dan.

"What are you doing here?"

Before Mr. Wilson could speak, the door at the

back of the shop flew open.

The lights came on.

"What is all this noise?

Get out, or I will call the police!"

This time it was Dad's voice.

He and Mom stood there in their night clothes.

Dad held a rolling pin from the kitchen.

He held it out like a weapon.

"Dad!" cried Dan.

"It is me!"

"And it is me, too," said Mr. Wilson.

"What are you doing here?" Mom asked Dan.

"What are you doing here?" Dad asked Mr. Wilson.

"It is his shop," Dan said.

"He can come here any time he chooses."

"We thought that there were thieves in the shop," said Mom.

"You had a good idea, Dan.

You raised the alarm."

"There is no need to worry about thieves," said Mr. Wilson.

Mom and Dad nodded.

Dad put down the rolling pin.

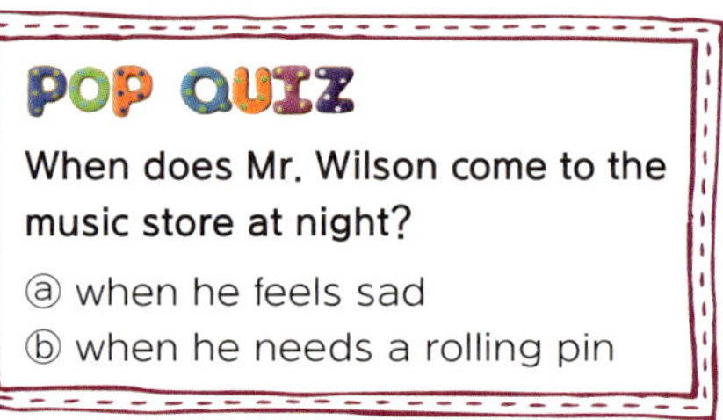

KEY WORDS

- choose
- have a good idea (*cf.* idea)
- worry about
- nod
- put down
- at night

Dan looked at Mr. Wilson.

"Why did you come here at night?" he asked.

"Sometimes, I come here at night when I feel sad," explained Mr. Wilson.

"I sit and I think until I feel better. I look at the mouse orchestra. I remember my wife."

Dan wanted to tell everyone about the mice.

But he thought that it would sound silly.

Then, he had an idea.

"Switch the lights off for a moment," he said.

"There is something that I want to show you."

Dad looked puzzled.

But he nodded, and switched off the lights.

The cloud had moved away.

Moonlight shone through the window.

It shone onto the Moonlight Orchestra.

At first, nothing happened.

Then, there was a tiny cough.

There was a ripple of music from the harp.

Mom and Dad gasped.

Mr. Wilson watched with wide eyes as Monty
blew his trumpet.

"I do not believe it," said Mr. Wilson.

"How can this happen?
I have not switched it on."

"It must be magic," whispered Dan.

"It is the magic of music."

The brass section played some music.

Then, the stringed instruments joined in.

"Now the woodwind instruments will play,"

explained Mr. Wilson. **Aha!**

"They are instruments that you blow into.

But they are not like brass instruments.

They have different mouthpieces."

▲ performers playing the woodwind instruments
(from top left, a flute, a clarinet, an oboe, and a bassoon)

KEY WORDS

- woodwind instrument
- different
- closely
- flute
- oboe
- clarinet
- bassoon
- make sure
- in tune
- sound right

Dan looked closely.

There was an oboe, and a clarinet.

There was a tiny flute.

There was also a long instrument that made a low note.

"That is a bassoon," explained Mr. Wilson.

"All the mice are making sure that their instruments are in tune.

Then, they will sound right when they all play together."

▲ a timpani, one of the percussion instruments

Monty held out his paws. The orchestra became quiet. He bowed to Mr. Wilson.

"Will you be our conductor, sir?"

A mouse stood by some enormous drums.

He dropped a drumstick.

It fell onto the biggest drum.

There was a *BOOM*, like thunder.

"Sorry," he said.

Mr. Wilson smiled.

"I see that the percussion section is ready," he said. (Aha!)

"Percussion?" said Dan.

"Instruments that you hit with something," explained Mr. Wilson.

"Drums and cymbals are percussion instruments."

KEY WORDS

- bow to
- conductor (cf. conduct)
- sir

- enormous
- boom
- thunder

- percussion
- cymbal

Monty looked up at Mr. Wilson.

Mr. Wilson picked up a stick from the window display.

"This is my conductor's baton," he said to Dan.

"I shall use it to show the musicians what to do."

The mice watched Mr. Wilson closely.

He waved his baton and they began to play.

When all the orchestra played together, it sounded amazing.

Each instrument had its part to play.

The low notes and the high notes mixed together perfectly.

The music sounded happy to begin with.

Then, it began to sound sad.

Then, it was grand and loud.

It made Dan feel as though he had just won a great battle.

The music faded away.

"Do you see?" said Mr. Wilson.

"We need sad music *and* happy music.

Both of them are important.

Both are beautiful in their own way."

Dan knew that Mr. Wilson was right.

He felt better already! 

"I have decided to join an orchestra," said Dan.

"Then, I will make new friends."

"That is a good idea," said Mr. Wilson.

"It will help you to feel better."

KEY WORDS

- fade away
- both
- important
- in one's own way
- already
- decide
- have tea
- teach (teach-taught-taught)
- spread

"Will you come and have tea with us tomorrow?"
said Mom.

"You can play your violin for us.

You can teach Dan all about music."

A huge smile spread over Mr. Wilson's face.

"Thank you," he said.

"I would like that very much."

Monty squeaked and waved his paws about.

"What is it, Monty?" asked Dan.

"If you join an orchestra, which instrument will you play?" asked Monty.

"I do not think that the violin will do.

I do not think that the trumpet will do."

Dan smiled.

He tapped two drumsticks together.

"I have chosen my instrument," he said.

"I will play the drums!"

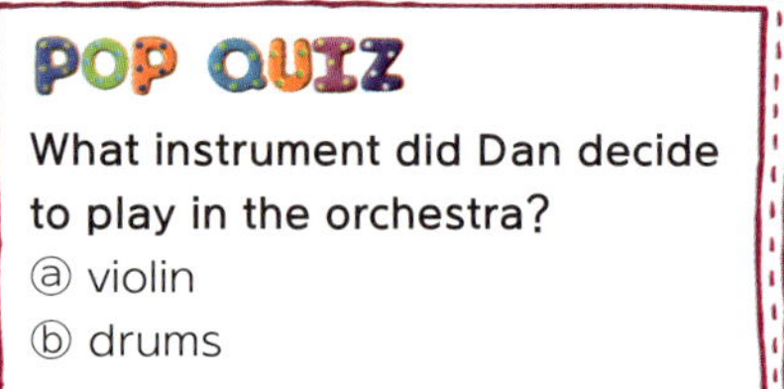

KEY WORDS

- squeak
- do (do-did-done)
- tap

Chapter Four Comprehension Quiz

 **A** Choose the best answer to each question.

❶ Why did Mr. Wilson go to the shop at night?

a) to play his violin

b) to fix the Moonlight Orchestra

c) to think about his wife and feel better

d) to teach Dan how to play the drums

❷ Which is NOT a woodwind instrument?

a) oboe

b) flute

c) drum

d) bassoon

❸ Why did Dan want to join an orchestra?

a) to learn how to play the violin

b) to make some new friends

c) to be the conductor

d) to play music with the mice

B Solve the crossword puzzle.

❸ The door c _______ ed open.

❺ Mr. Wilson looks at the mouse o _______ at night.

❻ S _______ the lights off for a moment.

❶ Dad held out the rolling pin like a w _______ .

❷ Dan picked up the d _______ sticks.

❹ It is the m _______ of music.

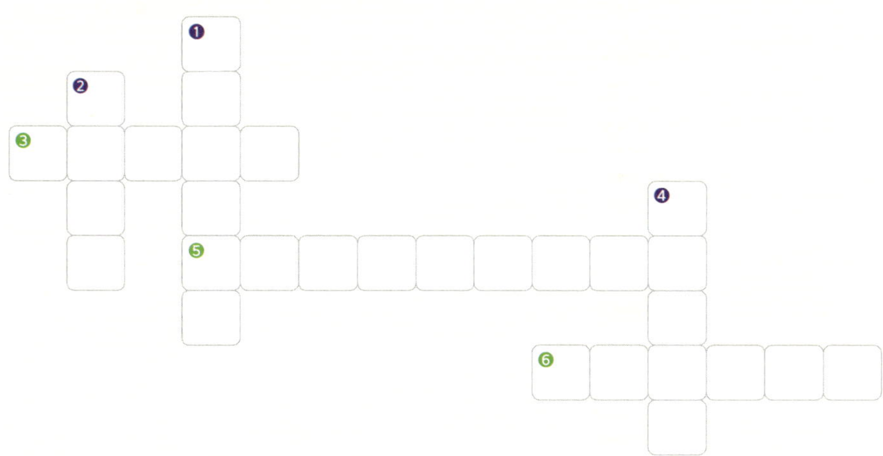

Let's Review the Story

Fill in the blanks to review the story.

Title: __________

Main characters:

D____, Mr. W______, Mom, Dad, and M______ the mouse

Chapter 1: __________ is sad. He does not like his new h______.

Mr. W______ is sad. He misses his w______.

Mr. Wilson shows Dan an o__________ made of toy m______.

Chapter 2: Dan wakes up in the n______.

He hears m______ and v______ coming from the shop.

He goes downstairs. He discovers that the mouse orchestra is a______!

Chapter 3: M______ says that the M______ O__________ wakes up when m__________ shines on it.

Monty shows Dan how to play some i__________.

Dan learns about the o__________.

Dan hears someone coming into the s______. He thinks it is a t______.

Chapter 4: The person coming into the shop is __________!

M______ and D______ come downstairs to the shop, too.

Dan shows them all the M______ O__________.

Mr. Wilson c__________ the orchestra.

D______ decides to join an orchestra and make some new f__________.

Let's Think & Talk

Think about the following questions and answer them freely.

❶ Have you ever watched or listened to an orchestra performance? How did you feel at that time? What impressed you the most?

❷ Is there any musical instrument that you can play? How do you feel when you play the musical instrument? If you don't have any musical instrument that you can play, what musical instrument do you want to learn to play?

❸ Do you have a favorite song or piece of music? Why do you like it? If you don't have a favorite song or piece of music, have you ever experienced that your feelings changed after you listened to any kind of music? Tell us under what circumstances you listened to the music, what music you listened to and how your feelings changed in detail.

Let's Review the Story

Title: The Moonlight Orchestra

Main characters:

D**an** , Mr. **Wilson** , Mom, Dad, and **Monty** the mouse

Chapter 1: **Dan** is sad. He does not like his new **home** .
Mr. **Wilson** is sad. He misses his **wife** .
Mr. Wilson shows Dan an **orchestra** made of toy **mice** .

Chapter 2: Dan wakes up in the **night** .
He hears **music** and **voices** coming from the shop.
He goes downstairs. He discovers that the mouse orchestra is **alive** !

Chapter 3: **Monty** says that the **Moonlight** **Orchestra** wakes up when **moonlight** shines on it.
Monty shows Dan how to play some **instruments** .
Dan learns about the **orchestra** .
Dan hears someone coming into the **shop** . He thinks it is a **thief** .

Chapter 4: The person coming into the shop is **Mr. Wilson** !
Mom and **Dad** come downstairs to the shop, too.
Dan shows them all the **Moonlight** **Orchestra** .
Mr. Wilson **conducts** the orchestra.
D**an** decides to join an orchestra and make some new **friends** .

After-reading Test

- The Moonlight Orchestra
- Level 2
- 20 Questions

  (Vocabulary 5 / Reading Comprehension 10 /

  Sentence Structure & Grammar 5)

1. Which of the following is NOT a pair of opposites?

    ① pull − push

    ② low − high

    ③ tight− loose

    ④ tiny − below

2. Which of the following pair has the wrong plural form of the noun?

    ① mouse − mice

    ② foot − feet

    ③ thief − thiefs

    ④ note− notes

3. Which one best explains what the "pitch" of a note is?

    ① how high or low it is

    ② how loud or quiet it is

    ③ how fast or slow it is

    ④ how long it lasts

4. What is the underlined part in the following sentence called?

    The trombone had <u>a long piece of brass</u>.

    ① the bell

    ② the opening

    ③ the slide

    ④ the baton

5. What is the common word for the two blanks?

> • Perhaps Mr. Wilson had left his radio ____________.
> • I have not switched it ____________.

① on   ② out
③ into   ④ for

6. Why did Mr. Wilson NOT want to live in the apartment anymore?
    ① He thought that it was too noisy.
    ② He wanted to move to a bigger home.
    ③ He wanted to make some money by selling it.
    ④ He did not want to live there without his wife.

7. What was the last thing that Dan heard as he went up the stairs?
    ① Mom calling
    ② Mr. Wilson playing his violin
    ③ traffic on the street
    ④ the door closing

8. What noise did Dan hear first at night?
    ① tiny voices
    ② a scratching noise
    ③ snoring
    ④ laughter

9. What made the mice wake up?
    ① the moonlight shining on them
    ② Dan opening the door to the shop
    ③ Mr. Wilson playing the violin
    ④ Monty sneezing

10. Which musical instrument had Dan tried to play once?
    ① the piano
    ② the guitar
    ③ the harp
    ④ the trombone

11. Which one describes a viola? Choose two answers.
    ① A viola is bigger than a violin.
    ② A viola is smaller than a violin.
    ③ A viola plays lower notes than a violin.
    ④ A viola plays higher notes than a violin.

12. What sound did Dan hear when the orchestra was silent?
    ① traffic
    ② a radio
    ③ footsteps
    ④ his heart beating

13. Who did Dad say he would call?

① Mr. Wilson

② the police

③ fire fighters

④ Mom

14. Why did the mice play their instruments before Mr. Wilson was ready to conduct?

① They did not want a conductor to tell them what to do.

② They had never played all together before.

③ They did not care what the music sounded like.

④ They wanted to make sure that their instruments were in tune.

15. What did Mom say when she invited Mr. Wilson to do something?

① Will you go to an orchestra concert with Dan?

② Will you come and have tea with us?

③ Will you make a new Moonlight Orchestra?

④ Will you live with us?

※ Choose the wrong part of each sentence. (16~17)

16.
He <u>hit</u> <u>the</u> drums as <u>harder</u> as he <u>could</u>.
  ① ②   ③   ④

17.
It made Dan wanted to cry.
① ②   ③   ④

18. What is the right word for the blank?

Dan was __________ surprised that he could not speak.

① too   ② than
③ so   ④ sure

※ Choose the correct sentence. (19~20)

19. ① His face looked sadly.
    ② His face looked sad.
    ③ His face look sad.
    ④ His face look sadly.

20. ① I used to live above this shop.
    ② I used to living above this shop.
    ③ I used to lived above this shop.
    ④ I used living above this shop.

Memo

Memo 

Sarah J. Dodd

Sarah J. Dodd is an experienced primary school teacher who resides in the UK, but has also lived and taught in Australia. She has a PhD in Science and a certificate in Creative Writing. She has published several books for children: "An Angel Anyway" (Anyway Press, 2008) the "Little Angels" series (Lion Children's Books, 2009/10), "The Lion Picture Bible" (Lion Children's Books, 2015) and "Legs: the tale of a meerkat lost and found" (Lion Children's Books, 2015). Her poetry for children has also been highly commended and published in the anthology "Let in the Stars" (Manchester Metropolitan University, 2014).
She is currently working on further picture books for the very young, and a novel for older children.

The Moonlight Orchestra

Written by Sarah J. Dodd
Illustrated by Yeseon Cho

First Published in August 2016

Editorial Manager: Juyon Choi
Editors: Juyon Choi, Kyunghee Jang, Jiyeong Park
Designer: Eunhee Lee
Cover Designer: Eunhee Lee

Published and distributed by

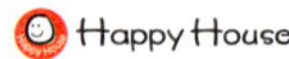

Darakwon Bldg., 64-1 Jandari-ro, Mapo-gu, Seoul, Korea 04031
Tel: 82-2-736-2031(ext. 250)   Fax: 82-2-732-2037
Homepage: www.ihappyhouse.co.kr
Publisher: Kyudo Chung

ISBN: 978-89-6653-409-8 18740 / 978-89-6653-156-1 18740(set)

[Components]
• 1 Audio CD (Recording Studio: Aram)
• Answer Keys & Korean Translation: Free download at www.ihappyhouse.co.kr